'I would recommend Michael's works to anyone within education, his yoga games are uncomplicated and the resources are first class! This book is user friendly, but also allows the reader to benefit from Michael's vast experience of not only teaching yoga, but successfully delivering within special educational needs settings. The games, sequences and postures within this book are suitable for both the beginner as well as experienced professionals.'

– Ryan Jones, Assistant Headteacher
at Treetops School, UK

'This is a masterpiece of a book for those teaching Yoga to children anywhere on the autistic spectrum. Michael gives clear guidelines as to how to engage the children's interest while considering the individual conditions of autism with structure and consistency. It works and is just brilliant.'

– Wendy Teasdill, Teacher Trainer
for the British Wheel of Yoga, UK

'This collection is another gem from Chissick. His structured and inclusive approach to yoga for those with autism is clear, user-friendly and most importantly, fun! There are so many ideas and approaches here that practitioners and parents will find invaluable. At a time when we are becoming increasingly aware of the lifelong importance of well-being and mental health for all, teaching yoga is a wonderful way to equip a vulnerable group of children with skills that will support their well-being for a long time to come!'

– Catherine McNerney, Assistant Headteacher
at Phoenix School, UK

'Amongst the expressive visuals and easy to follow yoga activities I've come to expect with Michael's books, you'll find some real life insights into engaging children across a broad range of sensory needs. I am by no means a yoga practitioner, but by following the game-led and goal-focused approach championed by Michael I'm able to confidently deliver activities that engage everyone in the class. It's no secret that children are more likely to be receptive to physical activity if it's fun but Michael's knowledge goes further by really considering the differing sensory needs of the children creating a balanced and nurturing environment. The structure and repetition of the activities breeds consistency, giving me the assurance of delivering a manageable, enjoyable, but above all achievable yoga lesson for all.'

- Phillippa Johnson, Specialist Lead Educator of Maths and Primary Classroom Teacher, UK

yoga for children and young people with autism

yoga for children & young people with autism

Yoga Games and Activities to Engage Everyone Across the Spectrum

Michael Chissick

Illustrated by Sarah Peacock

Jessica Kingsley *Publishers*
London and Philadelphia

Disclaimer: The author of this material is not liable or responsible
to any person for any damage caused or alleged to be caused
directly or indirectly by the information in this book

First published in 2019
by Jessica Kingsley Publishers
73 Collier Street
London N1 9BE, UK
and
400 Market Street, Suite 400
Philadelphia, PA 19106, USA

www.jkp.com

Library of Congress Cataloging in Publication Data
A CIP catalog record for this book is available from the Library of Congress

British Library Cataloguing in Publication Data
A CIP catalogue record for this book is available from the British Library

ISBN 978 1 78592 679 2
eISBN 978 1 78592 863 5

Printed and bound in Great Britain by Ashford Colour Press Ltd

Dedicated to
Veronica Armson, Stewart Harris
and Sarah Goldsmith for their trust
and support over the years

Acknowledgements

I would like to thank the following people for their honesty, encouragement and input: Angela Tuck, Veronica Armson, Sarah Peacock, Bob Insley, Kate Mason, Lindsey Walsh and Wendy Bataineh.

Contents

Introduction

I can walk into any class of children or young people with autism knowing that I will engage 93 per cent of them in the yoga lesson. It is not confidence, nor is it high self-esteem – heaven knows I don't have much of either. What I do have is a system that works, 93 per cent of the time.

The system, which I have developed over many years, is not only highly effective with children and young people with autism spectrum disorder (ASD), but also with children who have a wide range of related needs, including attention deficit hyperactivity disorder (ADHD), sensory processing challenges and difficulty managing their own behaviours.

This book is about my system and the structures that make that system work successfully.

Most books about teaching yoga to children and young people with autism tend to focus on those more able. This is hardly surprising, I suppose, because it is easier to teach *them* and it is certainly easier to write about.

This book is about how to include everyone on the spectrum, with an emphasis on teaching those with more complicated needs. It is also about how to include children with ASD in mainstream primary schools in the yoga lesson.

Such is the complex nature of teaching children on the autism spectrum and the diversity of abilities in any class or group, that whenever I go in to teach, I always have several plans up my sleeve.

Whether you work in school or in the community or you are a parent of an autistic child, this book will give you those plans, structures, games, goals, teaching tips and real working examples that you can relate to. My hope is that you approach your sessions with several plans up several sleeves, huge courage, a flexible mind and, above all, an unshakable determination to engage the children in front of you, come what may.

Who is this book for?

This book is a teaching guide for everybody who has been touched by autism and for those who will be. That means *everyone* in education, including special needs teachers, primary school teachers, elementary school teachers, teaching assistants, nursery teachers, speech and language therapists, lead teaching assistants and early years specialists – in fact, everyone who works with children with special needs.

It is also for parents with children on the spectrum who want to teach yoga to their children in a structured, fun-filled, down-to-earth way.

Of course, it is also for specialist children's yoga teachers who may already be teaching in special needs or want to make the leap, as well as people who want to teach yoga to children with ASD in a community setting.

Whether in mainstream primary or special needs, *Yoga for Children and Young People with Autism* is written for folk in or outside education who have little or no knowledge of yoga, as well as yoga folk who do.

That said, the more you know about your subject the better the teacher you will become, so if you do not have a yoga background, I hope this kick starts a deeper interest in this area.

Who this book is not for

This book is definitely not for people who need to read step-by-step instructions on how to do yoga postures. I have made it easy. Just look at the pictures of the postures. That will show you what to do. In some cases, show them to the children and they will see what they need to do. At this level, we are not looking for perfection.

Nor is this book for people who wish to include those aspects of yoga that carry a mystical or spiritual label. Aspects like chanting 'om' and teaching about 'chakras' do not, in my opinion, have a place in any form of children's yoga.

Finally, this book is not for folk who turn up in any teaching situation, and certainly in school, without a lesson plan or an understanding of classroom management skills, and who believe that they can 'sense' the needs of the children in front of them. As if!

And even more finally, it is not for adult yoga teachers who think they can turn up and deliver an adult-type yoga lesson.

Yet, maybe this book is for all the people mentioned, because it may open their eyes to another way. I live in hope.

A book of two educational settings

Most of the book is about how to teach yoga to children on the autism spectrum in special schools as a whole-class activity. That said, if you are a parent or carer using this book at home, I strongly advise you to stick to the structures and lesson plans provided. In other words, be guided by 'best practice'.

I have also written a section on how to teach children with autism in mainstream primary education. This is because there are more children with autism in mainstream education than ever before and numbers are increasing. Those children and other neurotypical children in their classes will benefit hugely from being included and it is important that you know how to do just that.

Differentiation across the autism spectrum

It is difficult to compartmentalize children and young people on the autism spectrum. That said, for the sake of explaining in the clearest of terms the *how*, *what* and *when* of teaching, I suggest that we gently shepherd them into three main groups, which we can call Maple Group, Oak Group and Willow Group.

Maple Group

Maple Group may comprise children who have very complex needs, who may have little or no verbal language and are pre-verbal. They are achieving below the expected levels of their age group in many areas and find it very challenging to interact or engage with others. Children in this group may roam or run around the room due to their sensory processing difficulties. Sitting for any period of time is not always in their best interests! They may be younger than the children in Oak Group.

Oak Group

Oak Group may be children who are at the expected language stage of development and therefore more verbal. They have developed more interpersonal skills, and work relatively well in group situations. Oak Group children will engage more readily and can follow more verbal instructions. They are more willing to work within a group and are more spontaneous in their language.

Willow Group

Willow Group may include children who have more challenging behaviours. They could be pre-verbal or at the expected language stage of development and have skillsets and abilities that are found in both groups.

Such is the nature of the autism spectrum that any child could at any one time be a member of all three groups. It follows, therefore, that a typical class of eight children in a special needs school will reflect that *membership* eight times, which makes teaching the whole class challenging.

Teaching children with autism in a special school

The two basic principles at the heart of my approach are:

1. Yoga for children on the autism spectrum is most vibrant and has the greatest positive impact when taught as part of the ongoing integrated school curriculum. This means that it needs to be timetabled weekly.

2. The best teaching method is a games approach. I find that all children, and especially those with ASD, are more engaged with the games approach than any other approach, largely because:

   - games are more structured than other approaches

   - yoga games are fun, so sessions are enjoyable

   - goals are easier to formulate and achieve

   - classroom behaviour is more manageable.

I honestly believe that the children I have taught with special needs have been more engaged, have improved their language skills, learned more social skills, have become better listeners and have begun to master basic self-control through my yoga games. For my part, it has been easier to plan, apply and achieve goals using the games approach. It's also great fun for adults and children alike.

It follows, therefore, that the strategies and teaching approaches offered in this book are based on yoga lessons that are:

   - part of the regular weekly timetable

   - delivered between 9.00am and 3.00pm

- practised either in the classroom or the hall depending on the overall abilities of the children

- involve whole classes, i.e. six to ten children

- have a high ratio of supporting adults to children.

**NOTE FOR PARENTS, NON-EDUCATORS
AND COMMUNITY WORKERS**

What is outlined throughout this book is simply *'best practice'*.
If you apply the same disciplines and principles when teaching your child at home or a group in a community situation, you will increase your chances of engagement and therefore success.

My overall aims

The greatest reward in my work comes when a previously unresponsive child steps forward to show that he or she wants to do the posture, knows how to do it, can speak his or her first word *ever*, can finish the line of a song for the first time, or can finish a counting sequence with an audible 'ten'. Such wonderful and moving milestones do happen in the yoga lesson. They are the cherries on the cake.

So how do you get to that point?

A piece of cake it is not! You must persevere. If there is one thing I have learned in my many years of teaching yoga to children with autism in special schools, it is this: *whatever happens, assume you are engaging the children and you will get to taste your slice of success.*

Continuing the cake metaphor, when I am teaching, I am highly structured. Within that structure, I target several layers or elements simultaneously; it's like a multi-tiered cake. Here are the layers:

1. Engagement

The main objective of the yoga lesson is to get the children to practise yoga postures. There are no benefits if the child does not take part in the lesson, which is why fun, enticing, whole-class games, like *Umbrella Game* and *Sneaky Trees*, are so important. In each game and, indeed, in each posture, the child is asked to react and engage; for example, by choosing a card in *Umbrella Game*, or standing still in *Tree Posture* and *Shark Game*.

2. Fun

There has to be an incentive for any child to get out of their chair or off their mat and do the posture or simply participate – *which is why there is always an activity built around the posture that makes the posture fun*. If children have fun in the posture or game, they will be more inclined to engage, stay in the posture longer and want to do it again and again, and, of course, remember it. For example, *Hoop Game* for the Oak Group or counting to ten in *Candle Posture* for the Maple Group.

3. Repetition

Repetition and reinforcement of games and postures over the weeks, months and even years (yes, years) are crucial. My lessons are highly structured with specific sequential activities that allow for postures to be repeated and reinforced. I always make an assumption that every child is getting *something* from the interaction, even if they are backing away or showing reluctance.

In fact, I suggest that in those cases, the key is to increase engagement and repetition. Over time, with gentle persistence, I have found that most children become more at ease with the postures, which leads to improved skills and greater competence, resulting in greater confidence. This is why I suggest that you stick to the same lesson plan, activities and postures over a long period and that any changes that you do make are small and incremental.

4. Achievement

Some achievement in the yoga lesson or session is my major goal for *every* child. This can be a 'big ask'. In the face of reluctance or lack of engagement, I break down the posture into simpler, smaller stages or steps, or I look for another way to involve the child. Whatever happens, I persevere. This is the reason I include guidance on how to help reluctant children in the chapter on postures (pages 90–112).

Any achievement, and I do mean *any* achievement, needs to receive lots of social reinforcement in the form of 'well done', clapping and cheering, pats on the back, or whatever is in line with your approach at your school or at home.

5. Social skills

Skills such as waiting, listening, speaking, helping each other, taking turns and following rules are learning outcomes by default in my lessons. There is a more extensive list on page 30. Opportunities to practise social skills will come up. You just need to spot them. If they do not, then I contrive to make them happen. For example, I may ask a child to help another in *Hero Posture* by supporting their outstretched leg. Perhaps a child is showing that they want their turn in *Candle Posture* immediately, in which case I may say, 'show me waiting' and come back to them. Of course, if that child has been reluctant on previous occasions, I will seize the opportunity to help them into *Candle* without delay.

I use songs with many of the postures, because this encourages and increases the child's language skills, helping memories and increasing the fun element. For example: Banana Song (page 44) and Hero Song (Yoga at School website; see Resources, page 124).

6. The postures

Fitness, flexibility and coordination and any other benefits will only come if children practise the postures. It will help you to know the specific benefits each posture offers. You can find that in the chapter on postures on pages 90–112. Each posture page comes with that information. Yoga at this level is not about perfection in the posture, but rather children simply doing their best on the day.

7. Adult support

One of the pillars to the success and positive impact of the yoga lies squarely with the teaching staff. In schools where I have trained the staff, I encourage class teachers and teaching assistants to timetable a weekly 30-minute yoga lesson at the same time each week; to do their best to make sure that the lesson is delivered with enthusiasm and pace; to ensure that everyone is challenged and achieves; and, above all, to create a great sense of fun around the lesson.

Teaching staff and parents will find themselves:

- modelling postures

- assisting children in postures and sequences

- singing the songs that accompany the postures and activities.

They will also encourage children to:

- work independently

- anticipate movement

- wait their turn

- complete the lines of a song and join in songs.

8. Sensory needs

There are two main sensory systems addressed in children's yoga:

- Vestibular

- Proprioceptive.

The vestibular system is the 'King of Sensory' (Delaney 2009). The main receptor for the vestibular system is found in the inner ear, where it tells us if we are moving or still and coordinates movement, vision, hearing and balance (Yack, Acquilla and Sutton 2002).

Our proprioceptive system depends on information received from receptors in muscles, tendons, ligaments, joints and connective tissue. A proprioceptive system that is working to plan gives us an 'unconscious awareness of our body position' (Yack *et al.* 2002, p.48). A combination of both systems gives us vital information about body awareness, movement, gravity, head position, coordination and where we are in relation to, for example, the floor and other people and objects (Yack *et al.* 2002).

Most children have vestibular and proprioceptive systems that are developing normally. However, some children on the autism spectrum have vestibular and proprioceptive systems that are dysfunctional, and this can affect their development. A child that is *hyper*sensitive to movement, for example, avoids movement and exercise, the lack of which can seriously affect both cognitive and physical development, not to mention gross motor skills and motor planning. It can also impact negatively on social skills, since the child may be unwilling to join in physical games in the playground (Yack *et al.* 2002).

A hypersensitive child may also suffer from 'gravitational insecurity' (Yack *et al.* 2002), which may manifest in not liking heights or having their feet off the ground.

Conversely a child who is *hypo*sensitive to movement will crave movement, is always on the go and finds it tough to pay attention (Yack *et al.* 2002).

Practising yoga postures can help to regulate these dysfunctions. Whether the child is hyper- or hyposensitive to movement, the yoga postures allow you to ease the child into the posture in the way that best targets their specific need (Goldberg 2013).

Thus in the case of a hypersensitive child, you are slowly and patiently easing them into the posture so that over the weeks and months you encourage more movement, whereas your work with a hyposensitive child will see you targeting less movement and more calmness in the posture.

Inverted or upside-down postures like *Candle* can be a first step to dealing with 'gravitational insecurity' (Yack *et al.* 2002). Best practice would be to place a cushion or foam block under the head to make the child feel higher and therefore more secure and at ease. Combine that with lots of encouragement to lay the head on the cushion or block. In addition, counting to ten is not only helpful in terms of engagement and counting skills, 'it provides a structure and creates predictability, something that children especially with autism crave' (Sutton 2013).

Inverted postures, like *Candle*, are excellent for regulating the proprioceptive system, because moving and adjusting limbs in an upside-down position involves lots of information processing (Goldberg 2013).

The same applies to postures that involve balance. When balancing, children are learning to shift weight from one leg to another and coordinate eye–hand movement, each of which, again, involves lots of information processing (Goldberg 2013). *Hero* and *Tree Postures* are both good examples of this. Many yoga postures demand a degree of balance.

Yoga postures flex, extend, compress and stretch muscles and joints, which again involves lots of information processing and therefore contributes to regulating the proprioceptive system (Goldberg 2013).

Structure

If you want to be successful teaching yoga to children on the autism spectrum then the answer is simple:

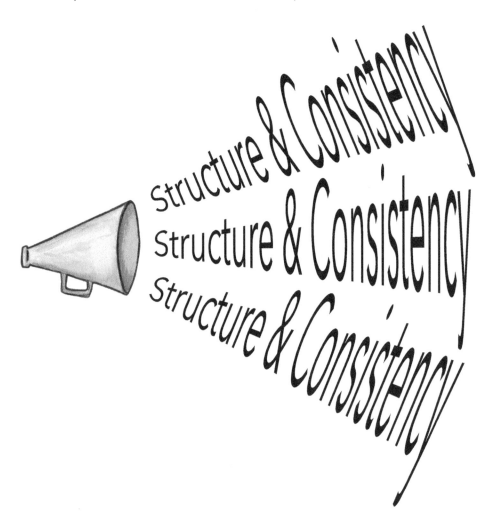

(I think you get the point.)

Structure in the yoga lesson includes the following elements whether in school, at home or in the community:

- The stages of the lesson/session

- Timetabling (and timing)

- Lesson/session location

- Set-up (chairs or mats)

- Using a visual timetable.

The stages of the lesson/session

The stages that I use, for example with Maple Group, are simple and fall into the following headings:

- Opening (main activity)

- Sequence

- Additional activity

- Relaxation

- Ending.

You can see how this works in practice with lesson plans A and B on page 33.

The stages that I use with more able groups like Oak and Willow Groups differ slightly and fall into the following headings:

- Beginning

- Sequence

- Main activity

- Calming

- Relaxation

- Plenary

- Ending and exit.

You can see how this works with lesson plans C and D on pages 34–35.

Can you see how I have changed the order of the first and third stage, and have excluded the calming stage with Maple Group children? This is because with the Maple Group, your opening activity *must be highly engaging - it has to be an absolute ding-dong attention grabber!* With more able groups, like the Oak Group, you can afford a softer, calmer and more thoughtful lesson beginning; for example, you might want to start with everyone sitting quietly in *Good Sitting*.

For each stage, you can choose a game or activity that will achieve whatever you are trying to achieve. It is as simple as that. For example, in the Opening stage for the Maple Group when your main objective is to grab their attention, you could choose *Umbrella Game*.

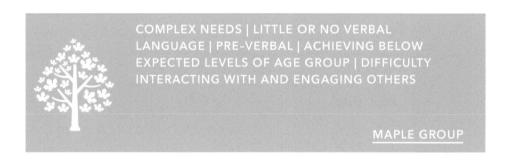

COMPLEX NEEDS | LITTLE OR NO VERBAL LANGUAGE | PRE-VERBAL | ACHIEVING BELOW EXPECTED LEVELS OF AGE GROUP | DIFFICULTY INTERACTING WITH AND ENGAGING OTHERS

MAPLE GROUP

Table 1 shows the stages of the lesson for the Maple Group with examples of games or activities and an idea of timing.

Table 1: Maple Group lesson structure

Stage	Example game/activity	Timing in minutes
Opening	Umbrella Game	8
Sequence	Sun Game	5
Additional activity	Circles Game	2
Relaxation	Bird	5
Ending	Rewards/Yoga is finished	3

Table 2 shows the stages of the lesson for Oak Group with examples of games or activities and an idea of timing.

Table 2: Oak Group lesson structure

Stage	Example game/activity	Timing in minutes
Beginning	Good Sitting	2
Sequence	Sun Game/Sun Sequence	5
Main activity	Sneaky Trees/Shark Game/Hoop Game	7
Calming	Rainstick Game	3
Relaxation	Ladybird Relaxation	5
Plenary	What did you like best?	3
Ending and exit	Strategy for lining up quietly and returning to classroom	3

Timetabling and timing

A 30-minute session, scheduled at a regular weekly slot, is the ideal. There will be opportunities to use elements of the yoga lesson at other appropriate times in the school day or at home. For example, using *Bird* as a calming activity or lining up for lunch in *Stick Posture,* or sitting in assembly in *Good Sitting.*

Lesson/session location

Location is central to the structure of a lesson. For example, invariably with Maple and Willow Groups, I work in their classroom. This makes sense because the children are familiar with their surroundings and because I am coming to them there are few, if any, transition problems. With Oak Groups, I may work with them in the hall or sports hall or a large designated room, although it may be appropriate to work with Oak Groups in their classroom. I assess the class in the light of the 'membership' of each group and decide which is the best place to work.

Set-up

If I am working in the classroom I have the children and support staff seated in a circle or semi-circle of chairs. This serves several purposes:

- Children are less inclined to run around, because the workspace is enclosed.

- It is easier for children to return to their chairs when they have completed the posture or activity.

- It is easier to manage children waiting for their turn.

- Children have an awareness that their peers are taking turns in the posture or game, which is an important goal.

- Class teachers and teaching assistants, and parents at home, can sit next to their designated child and help them when necessary.

- The activities take place in the area within the circle of chairs.

Using yoga mats can lead to complications, certainly with Maple Groups and some children in Willow Groups and maybe some children in Oak Groups. There is no precise answer to this. My advice is start with chairs in the classroom. Then after a while, depending on the needs of your group, try mats. If they find mats too difficult, revert to our circle of chairs.

Generally, with Oak Groups, as previously mentioned, I would tend to be working with them in the hall or a large room, and would have set up colourful mats in a circle. The circle helps with your classroom management because you can see everything that's happening and the children can see you. Have three or four mats in the centre of the circle that will serve as a demonstration area.

I encourage children to demonstrate postures in front of their peers because that helps build confidence and self-esteem. It is also a great way to teach or reinforce the posture without talking too much.

Teaching at home you will need to adapt these ideas. If you can involve siblings and other family members, of any age, that will create a more fun atmosphere.

Using a visual timetable

A visual timetable is a key structure in my yoga lessons. The idea is simple: children can see *what* they will be doing and *when* they will be doing it. This is particularly important for children on the spectrum, providing the structure that children with autism are comfortable with.

Here is a picture of the stand that holds my visual timetable. I tend to position the stand in the same place each time, whether working with chairs or mats.

It was originally designed as a magazine or leaflet display stand, but I have adjusted it to suit my purposes. It folds down into a small bag so it is easy to carry into school, but the greatest benefit is that, when set up, it is lightweight and easy to move about the hall. This means that I can put it wherever the situation dictates.

Typically, my visual timetable consists of posture cards, which show the postures we will be doing, and game cards, which show the games that are to be played. Children can clearly identify which postures and games make up the lesson and the running order.

There are some situations when I do *not* use the stand. For example, if I do not have time to set it up. It happens. No one is perfect and in that situation, I will show each card as I go along.

'John'

I will never forget 'John'. At the time he was a Key Stage 3 (aged between 11 and 14 years) pupil at a special needs school where I teach. He was one of a large group made up of three classes of children mainly with ASD. John was a big chap and his movement slow and cumbersome. Every week, he would lumber in, look around and, after much coaxing, sit in *Good Sitting Posture*. I was never sure if he was truly engaged or even happy to be in yoga. One day, in my haste I transposed two posture cards thereby changing the order on the timetable. John became extremely upset, would not sit on a mat, charged around and eventually came over to the visual timetable to point at my mistake. I simply changed their positions and John was himself again.

I learned *two* important lessons from that:

1. Never underestimate the power of a visual timetable when teaching children with special needs - especially children with ASD.

2. Always assume that children are interacting with the visual timetable, even if they don't seem to be. Apply this maxim to *all* children but especially to those with sensory and neurological impairments.

Consistency

Whether in school, at home or in the community, *consistency* in this context means programming the yoga session on the same day and at the same time *every week;* sticking to the same location; sticking to the lesson structure; having children sitting in the same places; using the same visual timetable each time; repeating and reinforcing the postures, songs and activities again and again and again as I have already mentioned; being consistent with your language, your praise, your rewards, your resources and encouraging your adult support to be consistent with their support and to be as consistent as you in the event that you cannot be there.

Aims, objectives and learning outcomes

Having clear aims and learning outcomes is an essential part of the structure of the lesson, especially when teaching yoga in mainstream schools (Chissick and Peacock 2017).

My aims

When I am teaching children on the spectrum there are specific aims and learning outcomes that dictate my teaching approach. I do not need to include them in every lesson plan because they are embedded in my approach and second nature to me now.

I discussed my overall aims on page 16 when I talked about simultaneously targeting several layers of a multi-tiered cake.

To recap, my aims are to:

- engage the children

- improve their social skills

- repeat and reinforce postures and activities

- give children a sense of achievement

- apply activities that target sensory issues

- and, above all, to have fun and to practise the postures.

At the same time, I will be using every opportunity to help children improve skills such as:

- concentration
- decision-making
- finishing number sequences, posture sequences and lines to songs
- following rules of the game
- anticipating what comes next
- self-control
- listening
- sharing
- assertiveness
- speaking
- participating
- taking turns
- independence
- teamwork
- leading the class
- waiting
- looking.

Specific goals

I show specific goals for each game. For example, in the *Umbrella Game* the goals are:

- Can I wait my turn?
- Can I sit in *Good Sitting*?
- Can I speak loudly?
- Can I join in with the singing?

This will give you an 'overview' of the aims of *Umbrella Game*. In addition, I give you goals for *each posture* within the game. For example, in *Hero Posture,* the goals are:

- Can I hold the pole?
- Can I stretch my arms forward?
- Can I stretch my leg back?
- Can I sing the Hero Song?
- Can I finish the Hero Song?

Some of the goals will apply to some children and some will not. For example, some children will be able to sing along with the song completely, some will only be able to finish the last sound of the song and some will only be able to hold the pole and stay in the chair. So, while you have general goals to guide you, they will become personalized in the lesson as you think on your feet and react to the needs of that child in that moment.

The greater the ability of the children the wider the range of goals that will be achieved. Success, however, is relative. Thus, a pre-verbal child saying 'ten' for the first time in *Candle Posture* can be as significant and gratifying to you as a very able child leading *Sun Sequence* for the first time.

Lesson plans

Finding good lesson plans that work with children on the autism spectrum is like finding a pot of gold. Welcome to yours!

I offer you four lesson plans, all of which are easy to implement, providing you structure the lesson as I have outlined on pages 22 and 23.

The plans are:

1. Universal plan A

2. Lesson plan B

3. Lesson plan C

4. Lesson plan D

Each plan is progressive, which means that you have the option to move your class or child or group onto the next plan if and when you feel the time is right.

1. Universal plan A

This lesson is ideal for everyone; hence I call it 'Universal'. The plan is suitable not only for children who may have very complex needs, but also for those who are more able. In other words, you can use this plan with Maple, Oak and Willow Groups providing you have set up your visual timetable, circle of chairs, have enough adult support and the children are in their classroom, or a suitable place if at home.

UNIVERSAL PLAN A		
Stage	Game/Activity	Timing (mins)
Opening/Main activity	Umbrella Game	8
Sequence	Sun Game	5
Additional activity	Circles Game	2
Relaxation	Bird	5
Ending	Rewards/Yoga is finished	3

Details of the games can be found in the Games chapter on page 37.

This lesson is also available as an animated video, which is available for you to download. You will find more details in the Resources chapter at the end of this book. On the video, you can see the lesson in action (with the exception of the *Circles Game*).

2. Lesson plan B

This plan is for children who fit between Maple and Oak Groups, so slightly less complex than Maple, but not quite Oak yet, but with sufficient verbal skills to master *Don't Be Sad*.

LESSON PLAN B		
Stage	Game/Activity	Timing (mins)
Opening/Main activity	Don't Be Sad	8
Sequence	Sun Game	5
Additional activity	Circles Game	2
Relaxation	Bird/Ladybird Relaxation	5
Ending	Rewards/Yoga is finished	3

3. Lesson plan C

This plan is for children who are more Oak Group. You will probably be using mats with this plan. However, if your children are not ready for mats then stick with the circle of chairs, making sure that there is ample room to work within the circle.

LESSON PLAN C		
Stage	Game/Activity	Timing (mins)
Beginning	Good Sitting	2
Sequence	Sun Game	5
Main activity	Sneaky Trees	8
Calming	Rainstick	5
Relaxation	Ladybird Relaxation	5
Plenary	Point to the game you liked best on the timetable	3
Ending and exit	Lining up in Stick, quietly waiting to go back to class	2

4. Lesson Plan D

This plan is for children who are very able, so Oak Group *plus*. You definitely will be using a circle of mats with this plan, and will probably be working in the hall, gym or a large designated room.

LESSON PLAN D		
Stage	Game/Activity	Timing (mins)
Beginning	Good Sitting	2
Sequence	Sun Game or Sun Sequence	5
Main activity	Shark Game	8
Calming	Rainstick	5
Relaxation	Ladybird Relaxation	5
Plenary	Point to the game you liked best on the timetable	3
Ending and exit	Bird, then lining up in Stick, quietly waiting to go back to class	2

References

Chissick, M. and Peacock, S. (2017) *Sitting on a Chicken. The Best EVER 52 Yoga Games to Play in Schools*. London: Jessica Kingsley Publishers.

Delaney, T. (2009*) 101 Games and Activities for Children with Autism, Asperger's and Sensory Processing Disorders*. New York, NY: McGraw-Hill.

Goldberg, L. (2013) *Yoga Therapy for Children with Autism and Special Needs*. New York, NY: W. W. Norton.

Sutton, T. (2013) 'Visual timetables.' *Special Education*, issue 216.

Yack, E. Aquilla, P. and Sutton, S. (2002) *Building Bridges through Sensory Integration*. Arlington, TX: Future Horizons Inc.

The Games

I have already made the point that the best teaching approach is a *games approach*. I cannot emphasise enough that all children, and especially children with autism, are more engaged with the games approach than any other.

The 13 games that I have chosen to include in this book work exceptionally well with children on the autism spectrum. With each game, I give clear guidance on:

- which groups the game is suitable for – Maple, Oak or Willow

- how to play the game for each group

- the stage of the lesson best suited to play the game. For example, Opening stage, Main activity stage or Calming stage

- the most suitable postures to use in the game

- the skills you are trying to nurture

- any resources you may need

- goals you are trying to achieve.

And in some cases, for example with *Shark Game*, how you can extend the game.

If you do exhaust the 13 games, there are many more to be found in my book: *Sitting on a Chicken. The Best EVER 52 Yoga Games to Play in Schools* (Chissick and Peacock 2017). Many of the games include songs. You can find more information in the Resources chapter at the end of this book.

Before you dip into the games, you may want to remind yourself of the characteristics of the children in each of the three groups. Here again are the details.

Maple Group – may consist of children who have very complex needs; who may have little or no verbal language and are pre-verbal. They are achieving below the expected levels of their age group in many areas and find it very challenging to interact or engage with others. Children in this group may roam or run around the room due to their sensory processing difficulties. Sitting for any period of time is not always in their best interests! They may be younger than the children in Oak Group.

Oak Group – may be children who are at the expected language stage of development and therefore more verbal. They have developed more interpersonal skills, and work relatively well in group situations. Oak Group children will engage more readily and can follow more verbal instructions. They are more willing to work within a group and are more spontaneous in their language.

Willow Group – may include children who have more challenging behaviours. They could be pre-verbal or at the expected language stage of development, and have skillsets and abilities that are found in both groups.

Opening and Main Activity Stage

Umbrella Game

What a game! This is one of the most successful special needs yoga games – ever! Playing it will create loads of opportunities to encourage Good Sitting and many skills including taking turns, waiting, joining in, completing sentences and making decisions.

STAGE: Opening or main activity
GROUP: Maple, Oak and Willow (mainly Maple)
POSTURES: *Banana*, *Candle*, *Chips* and *Hero*
SKILLS: Taking turns, waiting, listening, participating, communicating
RESOURCES: Umbrella, small posture cards, and game card. For details of the Umbrella song and the video of the Universal lesson in action go to the Resources (page 124)

Goals

- *Can I wait my turn?*
- *Can I sit in* Good Sitting?
- *Can I speak loudly?*
- *Can I join in with the singing?*

Make your umbrella...it's easy

First buy a safe children's umbrella. Hang the posture cards inside the umbrella. Each posture is represented by a set of two identical cards velcroed back to back.

What to do

Oak Group

Encourage children to be in *Good Sitting* in the circle, whether on chairs, the carpet or mats. Walk or skip around the inside of the circle singing the Umbrella Song twice:

Umbrella, umbrella, please choose me

I'm in Good Sitting

Can you see?

I tell the children that the umbrella is magic and that the magic only works when everyone is quietly in *Good Sitting* with lovely straight backs (this works a treat with children who can grasp that!).

Choose someone who is trying their best in *Good Sitting* (that's the incentive!). Hold the umbrella above their head and let them choose from the selection of postures hanging down from inside the umbrella. They simply pull off one card from the set.

I normally encourage that child to shout out the name of the posture because, for many, it is an opportunity to punch through their shyness.

The whole class comes into the posture, *or* children take turns practising the posture – whatever you feel is most appropriate and works best within the constraints of your space.

Work through the four postures.

Maple Group

The differences to Oak are that you will be:

- working from a circle or semi-circle of chairs not mats
- using *Umbrella Game* as your attention-grabbing opening activity
- talking less
- more dependent on other adult support to help some of the children through the postures.

COMPLEX NEEDS | LITTLE OR NO VERBAL LANGUAGE | PRE-VERBAL | ACHIEVING BELOW EXPECTED LEVELS OF AGE GROUP | DIFFICULTY INTERACTING WITH AND ENGAGING OTHERS

MAPLE GROUP

AT THE EXPECTED LANGUAGE STAGE OF DEVELOPMENT | MORE VERBAL | MORE INTERPERSONAL SKILLS | GOOD IN GROUP SITUATIONS | ENGAGES MORE READILY | ABLE TO FOLLOW VERBAL INSTRUCTIONS | SPONTANEOUS LANGUAGE

OAK GROUP

MORE CHALLENGING BEHAVIOURS | PRE-VERBAL | AT EXPECTED STAGE OF LANGUAGE DEVELOPMENT | HAVE SKILLSETS AND ABILITIES FOUND ALSO IN MAPLE AND OAK GROUPS

WILLOW GROUP

Circles Game

This came out of the blue when I noticed that many children with ASD, probably for sensory reasons, enjoyed moving in a circular motion. I cannot say that it is a yoga posture, or what it does for the vestibular and proprioceptive systems, but it doesn't matter, as it continues to engage the children and be a great success.

STAGE: Additional activity
GROUP: Maple, Oak and Willow (mainly Maple)
POSTURES: Sitting in chairs
SKILLS: Listening, participating, communicating
RESOURCES: Details of the Circle song can be found in the Resources (page 122)

Goals

- *Can I sing the song?*
- *Can I stop when we say STOP?*
- *Can I circle the other way?*

What to do

Maple Group

Keeping bottoms on chairs children move upper body in large circular movement. Stop on the STOP word then circle in the other direction and continue with the song:

Circles, circles

Circles the whole day long

STOP! CHANGE DIRECTION

Circles, circles

I'm singing my circles song

Repeat three times.

Note: Some children will need help with this. The best way is to stand behind the seated child with your hands on their shoulders. Apply a little weight and move their shoulders in the circular motion. Stop at the appropriate point and then circle the other way.

Oak and Willow Groups

If you are working on mats, have children spread and extend their legs out front and, singing the song, make the circular motions with their upper body.

Banana Game

This is such a simple game, yet an all time favourite because the children love *not* being caught out by teacher.

STAGE: Use as an opening or main activity
GROUP: Oak and Willow
POSTURES: *Banana*
SKILLS: Listening, participating, following the rules of the game
RESOURCES: Posture and game cards. Details of the Banana song can be found in the Resources (page 122)

Goals

- *Can I make a banana shape with my arms and body?*
- *Can I stop when my teacher stops?*
- *Can I hold the posture quietly?*

What to do

Oak and Willow Groups

Children stand on their mats (or in front of their chairs) in *Stick Posture*. Teacher demonstrates *Banana Posture* and sings the Banana Song:

I'm a banana

I'm a banana

I'm a banana, nana, nana, nana

I'm a banana

Oh I'm a banana

I'm a banana, nana, nana

Nooh

Explain that when *you* stop moving and singing *they* have to stop as well and stay in *Banana Posture*. If anyone continues to sing or move they will be *out of the game*! Most children will try hard not to be caught out. This wonderful side stretch is a terrific warm up. The song is very catchy too.

Maple Group

This may be too challenging for many Maple Group children.

Crown Game

This is a fun way to reinforce postures. You can also introduce new ones as long as you are prepared for the children to tell you: 'We don't know this posture!' Plus it's a great activity to encourage speaking and listening skills.

STAGE: Use as an opening or main activity
GROUP: Oak and Willow
POSTURES: All
SKILLS: Speaking and listening, thinking, participating, following the rules of the game
RESOURCES: Adjustable crown, posture and game cards

Goals

- *Can I identify yoga postures?*
- *Can I work well in a group?*

What to do

Oak and Willow Groups

Make or buy a simple headband or crown on which you can stick some Velcro. Choose someone to wear the special headband or crown. Choose a posture card that is familiar to everyone and attach it to the front of the crown using Velcro so that the wearer cannot see it. The class performs the posture and the crown wearer tries to identify the posture.

If the guesser finds it difficult, give them some clues until they guess the posture. Choose a new guesser and a new posture and go again.

Maple Group

This may be too challenging for many Maple Group children.

Don't Be Sad

Children can't wait to be the one with the sad face, so this is a good way to practise taking turns. This game can also trigger a little discussion about emotions with some of the more able children. Also, you get to practise four or five postures in one game.

STAGE: Main activity
GROUP: Oak and Willow
POSTURES: Opportunity to choose a variety of postures. For example: *Hero*, *Candle*, *Chips*, *Banana*, *Dragon*, *Stick* and *Boat*
SKILLS: Taking turns, waiting, listening, participating, communicating, concentrating and following instructions
RESOURCES: Posture cards and game cards

Goals

- *Can I make a sad face?*
- *Can I decide which posture to choose?*
- *Can I follow the rules of the game?*

What to do

Oak and Willow Group

Tell the class that you are pretending to be sad. Make a sad face. Everyone sings:

Michael, Michael

Don't be so sad.

What shall we do

To make you feel glad?

You reply, for example, let's all do *Boat Posture,* as that will make me glad. Then you all do the *Boat Posture.* The child next in the circle takes their turn to make a sad face, to be sung to by the group, and to choose a posture that will make him or her glad. Continue until you have completed five postures.

Extension

Replace 'sad' with 'grumpy' or angry. For example:

Michael, Michael

Don't be angry

What shall we do

To make you feel calmer?

(Doesn't have to rhyme)

Maple Group

This may be too challenging for many Maple Group children.

Hoop Game

Children adore this game. It's fast moving, addictive and I love it because we get to practise four postures in a short space of time.

STAGE: Main activity
GROUP: Oak and Willow
POSTURES: Choose four from your options: for example, *Tree*, *Candle*, *Chips* and *Frog*
SKILLS: Listening, participating, making decisions
RESOURCES: Four hoops of each colour, for example green, yellow, blue and red. Posture cards and game card

Goals

- *Can I perform the postures while quietly focused?*
- *Can I follow the rules of the game?*
- *Can I make good choices?*

What to do

Oak and Willow Group

Set up four hoops of each colour within the inner circle of mats. Introduce (teach) or reinforce the four postures to be practised in the game. Place each posture card by the respective coloured hoops. For example, place the *Candle Posture* card by the yellow hoops.

Have the children walking around the hall. When you yell 'Hoop!' each child chooses which colour, and therefore posture, to be in.

Another adult who has their back to the action will, on your signal, choose one of the four colours and give arbitrary points between one and five. Children in hoops of that colour will be very happy to hear that they have got points.

Carry on for another three or four rounds.

Alternative

Play an elimination or knock out game. It's the same as above except, for example, children in or around the yellow hoops are out of the game if yellow is called and will need to sit in *Good Sitting* on a mat. Eventually you end up with a winner. This will be fast and furious.

Maple Group

This may be too challenging for many Maple Group children, but give it a go with lots of adult input. I suggest that you have only *two* hoops inside your circle of chairs and that you work with only *two* easy-to-do and familiar postures. For example, *Banana* and *Chips*.

Place the *Banana Posture* card by the red hoop and *Chips Posture* card by the yellow hoop. Say 'Hoops!', helping any children who need help to a hoop and into the relevant posture.

Shark Game

This is a great favourite for the children and a highly versatile game for you. It's a game of contrasts: screaming to silence; fast movement to stillness and focus.

STAGE: Main activity
GROUP: Oak and Willow and some Maple (worth a try)
POSTURES: *Tree* and *Dragon* (Oak and Willow Groups); *Tree* only (Maple Group)
SKILLS: Balancing, focusing, self-control
RESOURCES: Posture and game cards

Goals

- *Can I make Tree Feet?*
- *Can I stretch up in Tree/Dragon Posture?*
- *Can I focus on an object in Tree/Dragon Posture?*
- *Can I put myself in the safest place on my mat?*

What to do

Oak and Willow Group

Have the children come off their mats into the 'water' – the floor area inside the large circle – and pretend to be swimming. Encourage children to use their shoulders and their arms fully. To avoid bumping, have everyone 'swimming' in the same direction.

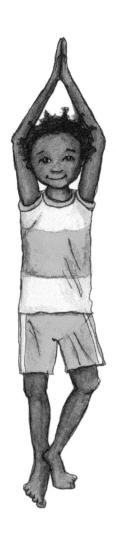

When you shout 'Shark!' each child will have to get to a mat and stand in *Tree Posture*, calmly focused. Anyone not on a mat or with a 'toe in the water' or talking has to go and lie down in the Shark's Dinner Table. This can be an area in the centre of the circle.

Repeat four times.

Extensions

- Alternate *Tree* and *Dragon Postures*.

- Include any postures you consider suitable. (Make sure the children are in postures that enable them to see and hear what is going on.)

- If you are using coloured mats, you could make a rule that no one is allowed on a blue mat, then purple and so on. Eventually you will have the children trying to stand calmly on three mats. This is excellent for encouraging them to share a small space. Alternatively, you could put bean bags on mats that are 'out of bounds'.

- Try tricking children to speak by asking questions.

Maple Group

This may be too challenging for many Maple Group children, but worth a try with lots of adult input. As you will be working within a circle of chairs and are restricted on space, I suggest that you use 240mm (9.5 inch) coloured circular base stations instead of mats. The idea is that when you shout 'Shark!' the children stand on a circular station in *Tree Posture*. *Tree Posture* is best for this game because children's feet fit well onto the circular stations. If you do add other postures, use those where feet or a foot can fit into the circular station.

Sneaky Trees

All children adore this classic game. This is the game that will reinforce **Tree Posture**, help children get to grips with balancing and encourage them to learn how to be still and focused. Without doubt, this game is the most popular and most effective yoga game in my world of yoga.

STAGE: Main activity
GROUP: Oak and Willow and some Maple
POSTURES: *Tree*
SKILLS: Balancing, focusing, self-control
RESOURCES: Posture and game cards

Goals

- *Can I stand in Tree Feet?*
- *Can I stretch my branches (arms up)?*
- *Can I stand very still and quietly focused in* Tree Posture*?*
- *Can I follow instructions?*

What to do

Oak and Willow Groups

Children stand in *Stick Posture* on their mats facing into the centre of the circle. Position yourself at the centre of the circle. Show the children how you want them to slowly tiptoe towards you at the centre, emphasizing the slow tiptoe movements. On the signal 'go', children tiptoe slowly forward. You call out 'Sneaky trees!' and children stop and come into *Tree Posture* quietly, calmly and in a focused way. Look out for opportunities to compliment children on the three important aspects of the *Tree Posture*: Tree Feet, hands stretching up, and their calm focus on a specific object. Repeat until children have reached you. Go back and start again.

Extensions

- WHAT ARE YOU FOCUSED ON? Position various interesting objects in their eye line that the children can focus on. Encourage them to focus on one of the objects when they are in *Tree Posture*. It makes it more fun if the teacher or parent has to guess which object a child is focused on.
- NAIL, TIGHTROPE AND MUD GAME: This is a big favourite. Repeat as above. Pretend that you have scattered sharp nails in the way and children have to act out what happens when they step on the sharp nails. Of course, when you shout 'Sneaky trees!', they have to stop and stand quietly focused in *Tree Posture*. Repeat with walking through mud or balancing on a tightrope. It is a game of great contrasts – the excitement of walking through mud, over nails and along the tightrope compared to the stillness and concentration in *Tree Posture*.

Maple Group

This is definitely worth a go with Maple Group children. You will need lots of adult input. Many children will find making Tree Feet difficult. Please persevere because the coordination and effort needed for this can be the start of improving the children's balance, body awareness and coordination and therefore improving their vestibular and proprioceptive systems.

Your circle of chairs will probably not be big enough, so find more space for this game. Don't waste time with explanations, just get on and enjoy it.

Spin the Posture

Children love being selected to be the one who spins the arrow on the board. Plus there is an element of silent, drawn-out suspense as we all wait to see where the arrow will land. Another plus is that you can involve five or six postures.

STAGE: Main activity (Oak and Willow Groups), opening activity (Maple Group)
GROUP: Maple, Oak and Willow
POSTURES: Choose five to six postures
SKILLS: Listening, and following the rules of the game
RESOURCES: Spinning wheel, cards numbered 1–6 (Oak and Willow Groups), small posture cards (Maple Group) and game card

Goals

- *Can I guess which posture the arrow will point to?*
- *Can I make a decision?*
- *Can I follow the rules of the game?*
- *Can I wait my turn?*

spin the posture

© Copyright Yoga At School 2016

What to do

Oak and Willow Groups

Set out six posture cards in the order 1–6 where they can be seen. For example: 1 - *Candle*, 2 - *Tree*, 3 - *Chips*, and so on. Velcro six number cards to the face of the spinning wheel.

Ask children to decide which posture they will do. On the shout of 'Now!' each child comes into that posture doing their best to remain silent, still and focused.

There is now a short period of absolute silence during which you spin the spinner on the wheel. When the number comes up, you announce it and award points, depending on the difficulty of the posture.

Repeat for another three or four rounds. See who has the most points. Do explain that it doesn't matter who has the most points as you are just having fun practising postures.

Maple Group

Arrange five or six small posture cards around the dial or face of the spinning board. Invite individual children to spin the arrow. The nearest posture card to the sharp point of the arrow is the chosen posture. This game is very similar to the *Umbrella Game*. The whole class comes into the posture, or children take turns practising the posture – whatever you feel is most appropriate and works best within the constraints of your space.

Tip: No spinner wheel? There are lots of creative and simple ideas for making one online. Or how about using a large die and calling the game: 'Roll the Posture'?

What's the Time, Mr Wolf?

This is a game of great contrasts – between the excitement and screaming and running around trying not to be caught, to the stillness and silence of standing in *Stick Posture*. Children also get to practise four or five postures, too.

STAGE: Main activity
GROUP: Oak and Willow
POSTURES: *Stick* is essential, and for example *Tree*, *Dragon*, *Banana*, *Chips* and *Frog*
SKILLS: Standing still, concentration, listening, self-control, following instructions
RESOURCES: Posture and game cards

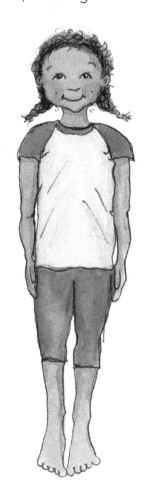

Goals

- *Can I be still and quiet in* Stick Posture *after being noisy?*
- *Am I alert?*
- *Can I follow instructions?*

What to do

Oak and Willow Groups

Stand in the middle of the circle of mats. Ask the class to make a circle around you. They are to ask you: 'What's the time, Mr Wolf?'

You reply, for example: 'It's Banana Time', meaning that everyone comes into *Banana Posture* singing the Banana Song.

Repeat with other postures, such as *Frog* or *Chips*. When you finally answer 'Dinner Time', everyone has to get to the mat to be safe from the wolf. Once on the mat, children need to stand still and quietly in *Stick Posture*.

Holding up the posture card helps, too.

If you tag the children before they reach the safety of the mat, they are out of the game and need to sit in *Good Sitting* on their mat.

Maple Group

This may be too challenging for many Maple Group children but do give it a go with lots of adult input.

Calming Stage

Rainstick Game

This is one of the most successful games to help children become still and calm. It works well because most children want to be chosen and the sound of the Rainstick in the silence of the class is calming and magical.

STAGE: Calming
GROUP: Oak and Willow
POSTURES: *Good Sitting*
SKILLS: Listening, sitting quietly
RESOURCES: Good quality long rainstick, or small plastic one, game card

Goals

- *Can I sit in* Good Sitting *with a straight back?*
- *Can I keep my eyes closed and listen?*

What to do

Oak and Willow Groups

Children sit quietly on chairs (or mats) in *Good Sitting*. Explain that you will only choose someone who has:

- a straight back
- their thumb and index finger touching
- a warm friendly smile (optional)
- most importantly, their eyes are gently closed.

Tiptoe up to someone who is doing their best to achieve those four attributes and invert the rainstick near their ear so that they can enjoy the calming and comforting sound of the 'trickling rain'.

Ask *that* person to choose someone who is also doing their best to achieve the four attributes, and invert the rainstick near their ear so that they too can enjoy the calming and comforting sound of the 'trickling rain'.

Repeat up to four times, asking children to be fair and not to choose their friends. Keep stressing that anyone peeping will not be chosen.

Maple Group

This may be too challenging for many Maple Group children. Nevertheless, try it with lots of adult input using a small plastic rainstick for safety. A big rainstick is not suitable for these children.

rainstick game

Relaxation Stage

Bird – Relaxation for Maple Group

This introverted posture helps children become calm and relaxed. It also stretches the spine and relaxes back muscles. It is handy to use any time in class to calm things down.

STAGE: Relaxation for Maple Group
GROUP: Maple, Oak and Willow
LESSON PLANS: A and B
POSTURES: *Bird*
SKILLS: Listening, thinking
RESOURCES: Game card. Details of the Bird Song can be found in the Resources (page 122)

Goals

- *Can I be still and calm in* Bird?
- *Can I keep my eyes closed in* Bird?

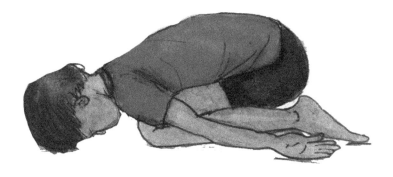

What to do

At the very end of the yoga lesson – the Relaxation stage – have the whole group, including adults, curl down in *Bird* for two to four minutes, singing the Bird Song:

> *I'm curling down in Bird*
>
> *I'm curling down in Bird*
>
> *Hey ho everyone*
>
> *I'm curling down in Bird*

Have each child choose a foam block or brick to rest their heads on as they curl forwards. Not only is this more comfortable, it also gives a point to aim for. Also, lots of gentle back massage will encourage children to stay in *Bird* for longer. If a child is reluctant to get off their chair and come into *Bird*, try holding the foam brick on their forehead and encourage the child to bend forwards a little.

Gradually reduce to a whisper and then to silence. Stay in *Bird* as long as you can. Then bring children out of the posture by touching gently on the shoulder and saying: 'Bird is finished… now sitting in our chairs.'

Bird – Exit Posture for Oak and Willow Groups

Bird is also part of the exit strategy for Oak and some Willow Groups - check back to lesson plan D on page 35. This is how it works:

STAGE: Ending and exit for Oak and Willow Groups
GROUP: Oak and Willow
LESSON PLANS: D
POSTURES: *Bird*, *Stick*
SKILLS: Listening, thinking
RESOURCES: Small pole, game card

Goals

- *Can I be still and calm in* Bird?
- *Can I keep my eyes closed in* Bird?

What to do

Oak and Willow Groups

At the end of the lesson, have the children come into *Bird* on their mats. Stay in *Bird* for a minute or so. Tap children on the shoulder with the small pole as the signal to line up by door in *Stick Posture*, ready to return to their classroom.

As part of my classroom management strategy, I have a special award that I give to one person in the group based on aspects such as behaviour, good listening, being kind, 'doing your best', good posture work and so on. I find that giving that award as they are lining up results in excellent behaviour and great *Stick Postures*. Very much the carrot, not the stick. Try it!

Ladybird Relaxation – Oak and Willow Groups

Your children will look forward to this, will complain if, for any reason, you leave it out, and they will forever tell you how they use this relaxation outside the yoga lesson. This is good news, because relaxation calms busy minds and young nervous systems, which in turn helps children deal with anxiety, tension and, ultimately, stress.

STAGE: Relaxation for Oak and Willow Groups
GROUP: Oak and Willow
LESSON PLANS: B, C and D
POSTURES: Supine (lying on your back)
SKILLS: Listening, being quietly calm, yet focused
RESOURCES: Ladybird finger puppet suspended on a piece of string about one metre long, Tibetan bells or triangle and game card

Goals

- *Can I lie still in* Ladybird Relaxation Posture *on my mat?*
- *Can I keep my eyes closed?*
- *Can I imagine the ladybird landing on my different body parts?*

What to do

Oak and Willow Groups

Have the children lie on mats on their backs with their arms by their sides, palms upwards. Make sure each child has enough space so as not to disturb anyone else. Show the children the ladybird finger puppet on string. Let the children know that the ladybird will only land on children who are lying very still with their eyes closed. Ask them to imagine that the tiny, shy ladybird is flying around the room and gently landing on them (the 'script' is below but feel free to change it to suit your children's needs).

The key

The key to this is to use a strong, yet warm, calm voice. When I introduce this technique, often for the first three to four weeks I ask the children to think about how the tiny, shy ladybird may be feeling, that any movement may frighten or startle the ladybird, and to show me how kind they can be by being as still as they can. It's a motivation that works well. Try it!

Structure and route

Other key aspects to this technique are that the ladybird takes the same route each time. It can be clockwise or anti-clockwise. Rarely do I use the words left or right because that can be confusing for many children. I prefer to use the words 'the other shoulder, thumb, toe' instead. By keeping to the structure each time, you reinforce the activity, which helps your children learn to an extent that they can practise this on their own at home or, frankly, anywhere.

Bells

I use small handheld Tibetan bells, which I ring each time the ladybird lands on a body part. The gentle sound indicates to children that the ladybird has landed and helps them focus on that body part, even if it has not landed on them. I ring the bells continuously to signal that the relaxation is finished.

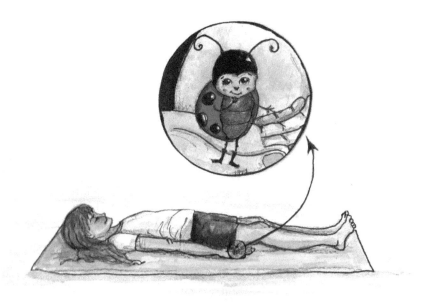

Expectations

Do set your expectations at realistic levels – there will be children who fidget to some degree. That's normal. You will find, though, that they are fidgeting a lot less than they normally would, and through regular practice, fidgeting and most movement will disappear – so persevere!

Note: This exercise works just as well in chairs as it does on the mat.

Ladybird Relaxation Script (Oak and Willow Groups)

A tiny, shy, tired ladybird needs to find somewhere safe to rest for a while. It looks down and sees you lying so still and calm. It thinks you look kind so it lands carefully on…

Your big toe, and stays for a moment.

Then the ladybird flaps its wings and flies in the air and lands gently on…

Your knee, and stays for another moment.

The ladybird flaps its wings again, flies in the air and lands softly on...

The tip of your thumb, and stays for a moment there, too.

The ladybird flaps its wings again, flies in the air and lands softly on...

Your shoulder, happy to stay there for a moment.

The ladybird flaps its wings and flies in the air and this time lands gently on...

The tip of your nose, and stays for a tiny moment sharing your stillness.

The ladybird flaps its wings and flies in the air and lands softly on...

Your other shoulder, and is so comfortable that it stays for another moment.

The ladybird flaps its wings and flies in the air and lands carefully on...

Your other thumb. It is so happy to share your calmness, it stays for a few moments more.

The ladybird flaps its wings and flies in the air and lands softly on...

Your other knee, where it stays just for another moment, very still, like you.

The ladybird flaps its wings and flies in the air and lands carefully on...

Your other big toe, and settles down quietly, calmly and happily.

Allow the children to relax in silence for between one and two minutes. Trust your judgement to bring them up when you think the time is right. Complete the relaxation by saying:

> *And then the ladybird flaps its wings and flies away, back to its home in the trees.*

Allow and enjoy a few more moments of silence as the children re-orientate themselves.

Ladybird Relaxation Script (Maple Group)

Ladybird Relaxation is not suitable for most Maple Group children. However, if you have been working with the group for several months, and have been following my lesson plan A, try the activity *in chairs,* at the Relaxation stage, and if it does not work then switch back to *Bird*, and try again a few weeks or maybe months down the line.

   With the Maple Group or any groups that may be between Maple and Oak, keep words to the absolute minimum. Thus the script will read as follows:

Ladybird lands on your big toe

Then your knee

Your thumb

Your shoulder

The tip of your nose

Other shoulder

Other thumb

Other knee

Other big toe

And then the ladybird flies away.

Sequences

What is the Sun Sequence?

The *Sun Sequence*, also known as *Sun Salutation*, *Salute to the Sun* (*Surya Namaskar* to yoga buffs), is one of the most popular and integral parts of any yoga lesson – children's or adult's. Simply put, it is a series of flowing yoga postures.

What are the benefits?

One of the objectives of the sequence is to move the spine in a variety of ways to increase flexibility. If you have tried it you will know that it exercises the whole body. Some people use it as their wake-up morning routine; others as a bedtime solution to help sleep. If you are short of time it can act as a whole session.

Apart from the fact that children love them, sequences are highly effective in lessons for several reasons:

- Children enjoy the security of the structure that sequences bring – they feel more secure knowing what is coming next.

- Sequences demand concentration and coordination.

- They provide opportunities for children to step up and lead the class or group.

- Children enjoy the flowing body movement.

- It is a more invigorating way to practise compared with isolated postures.

- Some children find sequences easy to remember and can teach them to friends and family members.

I have taught children *Sun Sequence* in every possible situation you can imagine. That includes children with the most challenging and severe physical needs, children across the autism spectrum, children with intense emotional and behavioural needs, early years children and the whole range of mainstream primary.

Sequences for children with autism

The sequence stage of the lesson is the stage where you have the greatest opportunity in engaging children with ASD in a whole-class activity because my sequences are:

- simple

- highly structured

- easy to remember

- easy to repeat and FUN!

Furthermore, by repeating the same sequence week after week, session after session children with ASD will feel more secure in knowing what is coming next and, in my experience, will engage.

I offer the following sequences for each of our groups, Maple, Oak and Willow:

1. *Sun Game in Chairs*: all groups, but especially Maple Group

2. *Standing Sun Game*: Oak and Willow Groups

3. *Standing Sun Sequence*: Oak Group.

In addition, I include four sequence games that you can play with Oak and some Willow Groups, once they have grasped the basics of the sequence. The games will help to reinforce the sequence and are great fun.

Sun Game in Chairs

Easy to learn, simple to teach and fun to do, this sequence also serves as a foundation for the more challenging sequences later. This sequence is specifically designed for children in Maple Group, but can be used with all groups.

GROUP: Maple, Oak and Willow
POSTURES: See diagram
SKILLS: Sequencing, leading, listening
RESOURCES: Game card

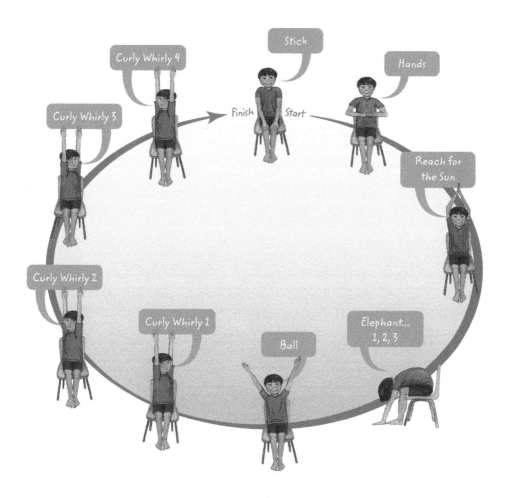

- *Can I follow the leader?*
- *Can I do the postures?*
- *Can I remember what comes next in* Sun Game?
- *Can I be the teacher in* Sun Game?

What to do

Oak Group

Children and adults are on chairs, for example, as part of lesson plan A. You lead the sequence by calling out the individual elements of the sequence in the order shown on the chart while performing that posture. The children, as a class, call them back to you while performing the posture too. For example: You say 'Stick' as you come into *Stick Posture*. The children call 'Stick' back to you as they too come into *Stick Posture*, and so on. You can slow or quicken the pace, increase or lower the volume of your voice, and even, after a while, lead in silence.

Practise at least three rounds.

Children leading

After a while, encourage some of your children to lead *Sun Game*. This may not be easy at first, and may need a lot of your input, but it is well worth it, so do persevere.

Maple Group

The same instructions apply as for Oak Group, except with some of your children you will need to hold their arms and, literally, take them through it. After a while, see if they are anticipating the next part of the sequence. Keep reinforcing this activity and have expectations that eventually many of the group will be able to perform this without your help.

Teaching tip: Over-emphasise each movement and the words that accompany each movement.

Standing Sun Game

This includes the same postures as *Sun Game in Chairs,* practised standing.

GROUP: Oak and Willow (Maple eventually, maybe)
POSTURES: See diagram
SKILLS: **Sequencing, leading, listening**
RESOURCES: **Game card**

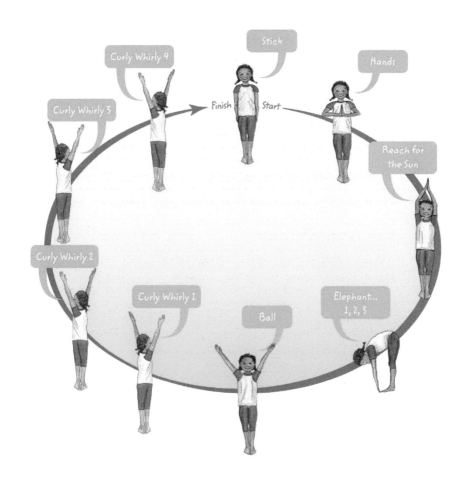

- *Can I follow the leader?*
- *Can I remember what comes next in* Sun Game?
- *Can I be the teacher in* Sun Game?

What to do

Maple Group

You will be making the leap from chairs to standing in front of chairs. You lead the sequence, as before, by calling out the individual elements of the sequence in the order shown on the chart while performing that posture. The children, as a class, call them back to you while performing the posture too. You can slow or quicken the pace, increase or lower the volume of your voice, and even, after a while, lead in silence.

Practise at least three rounds and then return to chairs to continue with the next stage of the lesson.

It is imperative to help some children with this sequence by holding their arms and, literally, taking them through it. After a while, see if they are anticipating the next part of the sequence.

Oak and Willow Group

Children and adults will be working on mats, for example as part of lesson plans B, C and D. As before, you lead by calling out the individual elements of the sequence in the order shown on the chart while performing that posture and the children call it back to you while performing the posture too. Remember, you can slow or quicken the pace, increase or lower the volume of your voice, and even, after a while, lead in silence.

Practise at least three rounds and then on to the next stage of the lesson.

Children leading

A few weeks down the line, encourage some of your Oak or Maple Groups to lead *Standing Sun Game*. This may not be easy at first for children in Maple Group, and may need a lot of your input, but it is well worth it, so do persevere.

Teaching tip: Over-emphasise each movement and the words that accompany each movement.

Standing Sun Sequence

This sequence has been developed for more able children, as in Oak Group, and is more challenging than *Standing Sun Game* and *Sun Game in Chairs* and includes more postures. *Sun Sequence* is a terrific warm-up activity.

GROUP: Oak
POSTURES: See diagram
SKILLS: Sequencing, leading, listening and following instructions
RESOURCES: Game card

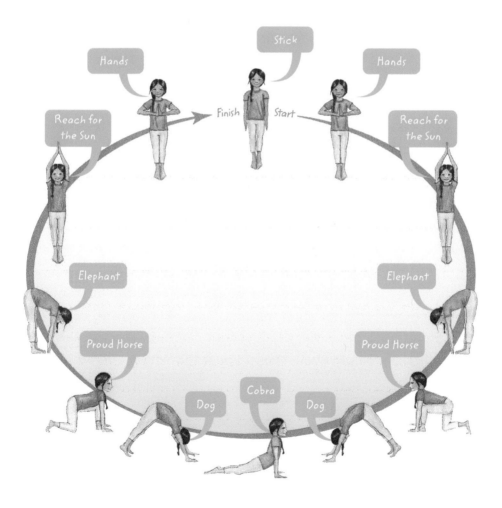

Goals

- *Can I follow the leader?*
- *Can I perform each posture?*
- *Can I remember what comes next in* Sun Sequence?
- *Can I be the teacher in* Sun Sequence?
- *Can I teach my friends and family* Sun Sequence?

What to do

Oak Group

Children and adults will be working on mats, for example as part of lesson plan D. You lead by calling out the individual elements of the sequence in the order shown on the chart while performing that posture, and the children call it back to you while performing the posture too. Remember, you can slow or quicken the pace, increase or lower the volume of your voice, and even, after a while, lead in silence.

Practise at least three rounds and then go on to the next stage of the lesson.

Getting started

I suggest that when you introduce this sequence that you teach the first *four* postures in the first lesson and the rest of the sequence over the next two lessons. If you are moving on to this from *Standing Sun Game*, the first four postures are the same so you might as well get stuck in and teach the whole *Sun Sequence*.

Children leading

After a while, encourage individuals to step up and take the lead. My guess is that you will be besieged with willing volunteers.

Sequence Games

Here are some games that will help to reinforce the postures and skills that the sequences offer and inject even more fun into your lessons. Admittedly, there are more games for Oak and Willow Groups than Maple Groups, but that is the nature of the beast. Choose your game and stick with it for at least five weeks because they are rich in enjoyment and learning experiences.

Chase the Frog

This game will keep children on their toes, aware that at any moment they could be asked to lead. I call it **Chase the Frog** because I use a frog-shaped yoga block, but you can use anything – even a sponge. So…chase the sponge, shoe, smelly sock…

STAGE: Sequence
GROUP: Oak and Willow
SUITABLE SEQUENCES: *Sun Game in Chairs*, *Standing Sun Game* and *Sun Sequence*
SKILLS: Sequencing, concentration
RESOURCES: Foam frog, shoe, trainer, beanbag, smelly sock

Goals

• *Do I know what comes next in* Sun Sequence?

• *Am I alert?*

What to do

Perform a round of *Sun Sequence* to reinforce the activity. On the next round, place the frog at the feet of a child. That child becomes the leader, until you pick up the frog and place it at the feet of another child, who takes over from the previous child at the correct place in the sequence.

Continue to the end of the sequence and repeat.

Yoga Detective – What's Missing?

This is a wonderful game to reinforce the **Sun Game** and **Sun Sequence**. It is also a great opportunity to encourage children to speak out in a group.

STAGE: Sequence
GROUP: Oak and Willow
SUITABLE SEQUENCES: *Sun Game in Chairs*, *Standing Sun Game* and *Sun Sequence*
SKILLS: Sequencing, concentration
RESOURCES: Game Card

Goals

- *Can I identify the missing part to the sequence?*

What to do

Tell the children that:

- you will lead but will leave out one part of the sequence
- you will decide which one to leave out before you start
- their job as detectives is to spot which posture is missing
- they have to wait until the sequence is completed before offering their answers.

Call out the postures for the sequence, leaving out one posture. When you've finished the sequence, choose three 'yoga detectives' to say what is missing.

Repeat once more.

Extensions

- Ask for a volunteer to lead. Remind them they need to decide which posture they will leave out of the sequence before starting.

- Ask the detective to demonstrate the missing posture instead of saying it.

Incredible Weather Game

Children love this game, especially in the summer, when they will do their best to be picked to be sprayed with water, cooled by the wind and shocked by the thunder.

STAGE: Sequence
GROUP: Oak
SUITABLE SEQUENCES: *Sun Game in Chairs*, *Standing Sun Game* **and** *Sun Sequence*
SKILLS: Sequencing, concentration
RESOURCES: Clean plastic plant spray bottle, large piece of foam or card, 'thunder' tube or something that makes a thunder sound

Goals

- *Can I continue with a sequence, even when it is hard to concentrate?*

What to do

Lead the sequence. At an appropriate moment, ask someone which weather they would choose from a choice of wind, rain or thunder. If they choose rain, spray them with a fine spray of water; if they choose wind, use something big enough to flap cold wind onto them. If they choose thunder, I shake a special 'thunder tube' that I bought in a toyshop. You will find that the children will work hard to be chosen.

Continue with the sequence, stopping frequently to choose the next new 'victim'.

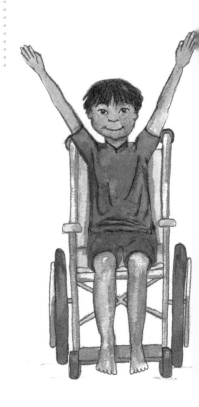

One Behind

This is a terrific concentration builder as well as one of those games where children love to rise to the bait that challenges their powers of concentration.

STAGE: Sequence
GROUP: Oak
SUITABLE SEQUENCES: *Sun Game in Chairs*, *Standing Sun Game* and *Sun Sequence*
SKILLS: Sequencing, concentration
RESOURCES: Game card

Goals

• *Can I completely concentrate on the sequence?*

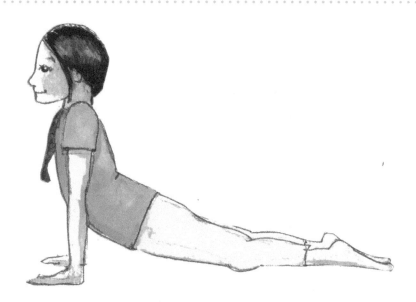

What to do

It is best to play this when the children know either the *Sun Game* or the *Sun Sequence* inside out.

Explain to the class or group that you will lead the sequence; that you will begin with *Stick*, but they will do and say nothing. Then, when you have said *Hands*, they come into *Stick*. When you say and come into *Reach for the Sun* they come into *Hands*. In other words, they will be *one behind*.

When it comes to the final instruction, it is a good idea to say, 'And nothing' or 'And blah blah' as their cue to say, 'And *Stick*'.

This may take several attempts to get close, so persevere.

Extensions

- Ask one of the children to lead the class or group.
- Try playing *Two Behind*.
- And if you are very brave...*Four and Five Behind*!

The Postures

Below are details of postures that you can use with children and young people across the autism spectrum. With each posture is guidance about:

- which games the postures are best suited for

- what activity to weave around the posture

- how to modify the postures to help individual children

- what action to take if a child is reluctant to perform the posture.

There are not blow-by-blow instructions on how to perform the postures. You only have to look at the illustration to know what to do, and at this level we are not looking for perfection. Of course, there are many more yoga postures out there, but I have kept to the 10, because they have been outstandingly successful in my career of teaching yoga to children on the autism spectrum, especially those in Maple Group.

Another reason to stick to the 'Magnificent 10' is that reinforcing the same postures over and over again makes the children so familiar with them that they will have little or no resistance to performing each posture. Many children on the spectrum, remember, work best when they know what's coming next. Again, I am thinking about the Maple Group, but the same will apply to some children in Oak and Willow Groups.

Introduce new postures by all means, but do so in small increments and then reinforce, reinforce and reinforce some more.

If you want to increase your arsenal of postures, you can go to my website where you can buy 30 posture cards which will include the 10 listed here plus another 20 popular children's yoga postures. There are more details in the Resources section on page 122.

Before you dip into the Postures chapter, you may want to remind yourself again of the characteristics of the children in each of the three groups:

Maple Group – may consist of children who have very complex needs; who may have little or no verbal language and are pre-verbal. They are achieving below the expected levels of their age group in many areas and find it very challenging to interact or engage with others. Children in this group may roam or run around the room due to their sensory processing difficulties. Sitting for any period of time is not always in their best interests! They may be younger than the children in Oak Group.

Oak Group – may be children who are at the expected language stage of development and therefore more verbal. They have developed more interpersonal skills, and work relatively well in group situations. Oak Group children will engage more readily and can follow more verbal instructions. They are more willing to work within a group and are more spontaneous in their language.

Willow Group – may include children who have more challenging behaviours. They could be pre-verbal or at the expected language stage of development, and have skillsets and abilities that are found in both groups.

Banana

This is an absolute favourite and such a wonderful side stretch, which stretches and straightens the whole body.

Games for this posture

Umbrella Game, Banana Game, Don't Be Sad, Hoop Game, Crown Game, Spin the Posture, What's the Time, Mr Wolf?

Goals

- *Can I stretch up to each side?*
- *Can I remember the Banana Song?*
- *Can I finish the words to the song?*

Resources

Details of the Banana Song can be found on the Resources page 124.

What to do

Banana is very much a whole-class activity. The activity is simple and great fun. Simply come into posture and, stretching from side to side, sing:

I'm a banana

I'm a banana

I'm a banana, nana, nana, nana

I'm a banana

Oh I'm a banana

I'm a banana, nana, nana

Nooh

Repeat once more.

Modifications and teaching tips

At first, you may have to help the children into the posture by standing behind and helping them to stretch their arms, as in the picture.

Reluctant children

If a child is reluctant, it may be that they are hypersensitive to vestibular stimulation or fearful of any common movements. Try the posture in their chair with slow careful movement, helping to stretch their arms above their heads.

Boat

This strengthens neck, back, tummy muscles, ankles and toes. You need focus and perseverance with this one because it's a challenging balance.

Games for this posture

Umbrella Game, Banana Game, Don't Be Sad, Hoop Game, Crown Game, Spin the Posture, What's the Time, Mr Wolf?

Goals

- *Can I rest my legs on the pole?*
- *Can I wait for my turn?*
- *Can I remember the Boat Song?*

Resources

Pole.

What to do

Boat is best practised one child at a time. The child sits on the floor. Because a certain amount of tummy strength is needed, you may need to help them rest their lower legs on a pole. Help the child extend their arms so that they can hold the pole. Over time, aim for child independence.

Sing: 'Row, row row your boat' or 'Yo yo yoga boat'.

Modifications and teaching tips

You may need two adults helping on this - someone to support the back and someone at the front with the pole.

Reluctant children

Try *Boat* in the chair. Gently raise legs and rest them on the pole. If that does not work, try the child holding the pole with their arms outstretched. You can sing the Boat Song gently moving the pole to and fro.

Candle

This strengthens legs, ankles and toes and is very good for circulation. It is also excellent for strengthening tummy muscles, and good for all round fitness and health.

Games for this posture

Umbrella Game, Don't Be Sad, Hoop Game, Crown Game, Spin the Posture, What's the Time, Mr Wolf?

Goals

- *Can I finish the counting by saying 'ten'?*
- *Can I lift my legs up myself?*
- *Can I keep my legs up myself?*

What to do

When you are introducing *Candle*, work with one child at a time. There will come a time when you will have nearly all the class in *Candle*, albeit some with adult help.

Initially, encourage the child to lie on their back with their head on the floor, as in the picture. Stand at their feet and encourage them to bend their knees and lift, first one leg, then the other. Hold the backs of the child's ankles so that the backs of the legs (hamstring muscles) are stretched as far as possible. Have the whole group count to ten. When you get to nine, stop and encourage the child to complete the count, i.e. say 'ten'.

Gently help the children to bend their knees and their lower legs to the floor, carefully avoiding feet in faces.

Modifications and teaching tips

After a few sessions, try having two or three children in *Candle* at the same time. Then if that is going well, try for the whole class. Just be mindful of feet and faces when they come down from the posture. Encourage children to bring their legs up and hold them in the posture themselves.

Reluctant children

Some children do not like being in an inverted posture or having their head or body on the floor. In those cases, let the child stay in the chair while you raise their legs as high as possible. Some children will like a cushion or foam block under their head. Above all, give plenty of reassurance.

Chips

Jumping and bursting with energy, this posture strengthens and stretches the entire body and best of all gets everyone involved. The activity is simple and great fun.

Games for this posture

Umbrella Game, Banana Game, Don't Be Sad, Hoop Game, Crown Game, Spin the Posture, What's the Time, Mr Wolf?

Goals

- *Can I stretch and jump at the right moment?*
- *Can I sing the Chips Song?*

Resources

Details of the Chips Song can be found in the Resources (page 124).

What to do

Simply sing:

> I love chips, I love chips,
>
> I love chips
>
> And tomato ketchup

As you sing the word *chips*, encourage the children to jump and stretch at the same time. As you sing '*...and tomato ketchup*', encourage the children to bend forwards to touch the floor with their hands, which of course is a forward bend.

Repeat three times.

Modifications and teaching tips

At first you may have to help the children into the posture by standing behind or in front and helping them to stretch their arms, as in the picture.

Reluctant children

Some children may find the shouting and fast action too much. If that is the case, slow the whole thing down and perform the activity quietly, one at a time. If it is too noisy for sound-sensitive children, then whisper the song.

Dragon

Dragon is about stability and working the muscles at the side of the upper body. I use this posture with more able children to work on perseverance and focus.

Games for this posture

Umbrella Game, Don't Be Sad, Hoop Game, Crown Game, Shark Game, Spin the Posture, What's the Time, Mr Wolf?

Goals

- *Can I put one knee up?*
- *Can I sing the Dragon Song?*
- *Can I stretch up to the ceiling?*

Resources

Details of the Dragon Song can be found in the Resources (page 124).

What to do

Demonstrate the posture and encourage everyone to join you in the song:

I'm in Dragon, I'm in Dragon

Look at me, look at me

Stretching to the ceiling

Stretching to the ceiling

Well done me

Well done you

Change legs and repeat.

Modifications and teaching tips

There may be some children who need lots of help with the leg/knee position or the arms stretching or both.

Reluctant children

This is difficult for some children to coordinate, which may be the source of the reluctance. Work on *one* aspect at a time to build confidence. For example, let the child stay in the chair and help them stretch up their arms. For the next stage, encourage the child to work on the floor with the leg/knee position.

Frog

This is a squatting posture, which means that it helps with the flexibility of knees, ankles and hip joints. *Frog* is also good for the back and tones the leg muscles.

There is lots of proprioceptive and vestibular stimulation too.

Games for this posture

Umbrella Game, Don't Be Sad, Hoop Game, Crown Game, Spin the Posture, What's the Time, Mr Wolf?

Goals

- *Can I bend my knees in* Frog?
- *Can I hop in* Frog?

None.

What to do

At first you may have to help the child by standing in front of them or holding their hands. Bend your knees as you go down into the *Frog,* encouraging the child to do the same. You may need another adult to help the child bend their knees. It is not always easy, but there are so many benefits, so do persevere. Once you are down in the posture simply say *ribbit, ribbit, ribbit* as you and the child bounce around in the posture for as long as possible.

Repeat two or three times.

Modifications and teaching tips

This is difficult for some children. Simply hold hands facing each other and try to get the child to bend at the knees. This may take weeks for some children, but since there are high proprioceptive and vestibular benefits from *Frog,* do persevere.

Reluctant children

Allow the child to stay in the chair. Hold hands and jump up and down, having fun in the spirit of the game. If the child is sensitive to noisy activities, then do it silently.

Good Sitting

This is one of the most important postures in your toolkit. It encourages children to be still and calm as they work on straight backs and sitting quietly. This is another posture where children can develop self-control.

Games for this posture

Umbrella Game, Don't Be Sad, Hoop Game, Crown Game, Spin the Posture, What's the Time, Mr Wolf?

Goals

- *Can I sit quietly in Good Sitting?*
- *Can I keep my back straight?*
- *Can I keep my thumb and index finger together? (Maple Group)*
- *Can I keep my hands on my knees?*

Resources

None.

What to do

Good Sitting on a chair

Good Sitting on a mat

Modifications and teaching tips

You cannot expect *any* child to be in *Good Sitting* for long, so use it as a posture that you return to in between other postures and activities.

Reluctant children

It is rarely a case of reluctance, but probably more about children wanting to roam or run around the room for all kinds of reasons. Sitting for any period of time is not always in their best interests! Make a judgement call or maybe move on to the next activity.

Hero

Most children love this posture. *Hero* provides a whole raft of benefits, including strengthening back, legs, shoulders and arms. The more you practise a posture that demands concentration, balance, coordination and perseverance, the more those elements become evident. Above all, it will engage 93 per cent of children.

Games for this posture

Umbrella Game, Don't Be Sad, Hoop Game, Spin the Posture, Crown Game, What's the Time, Mr Wolf?

Goals

- *Can I hold the pole?*
- *Can I stretch my leg back?*
- *Can I sing the Hero Song?*
- *Can I finish the Hero Song?*

Resources

- Details of the Hero Song can be found on the Resources page 124.
- Pole.

What to do

Offer the pole to the child in the chair. The majority of children will reach out, grasp it and stand. It is amazing how well this works. Encourage the child to raise one leg backwards, as in the picture. At first have another adult support that leg by holding knee and ankle, gently stretching leg backwards, while the person holding the pole will gently stretch the child's arms. So the overall effect is a gentle stretching of both arms and leg.

Sing the Indiana Jones theme tune.

Modifications and teaching tips

The pole is highly significant. If the child is readjusting their position, that is a good sign that something is happening. After a few sessions, look to see if the child offers their leg voluntarily.

Reluctant children

If a child is reluctant to leave the chair, encourage them to grip the pole at the very least. If a child is reluctant to lift their leg, try tapping the leg to see if the child is then encouraged to offer the leg. If not, help to bring the leg up. Some children will bring both legs up - great fun, but not what you are trying to achieve. In that situation *stop*, explain clearly that one foot is to stay on the floor, and start again.

Tree

This is one of the best postures to help children work on balance, coordination and strengthening ankles and feet as well as toning leg muscles. It helps to build up concentration and focus and provides lots of proprioceptive and vestibular stimulation.

Games for this posture

Umbrella Game, Sneaky Trees, Crown Game, Don't Be Sad, Shark Game, Spin the Posture, What's the Time, Mr Wolf?

Goals

- *Can I stretch my arms up over my head?*
- *Can I make Tree Feet?*
- *Can I sing Tree Song?*
- *Can I say the last word in the Tree Song?*

Resources

The Tree Song is available from the Yoga at School website (see Resources, page 124).

What to do

At first, you may have to help the children into the posture by helping them with their Tree Feet and stretching their arms, as in the picture. Then sing the Tree Song.

This is preparation for a time in the future when the children will be encouraged to play a lovely game called *Sneaky Trees*.

Modifications and teaching tips

It will help if you see *Tree Posture* as having *three* aspects.

Aspect 1: Tree Feet, which you will need to help many children achieve.

Aspect 2: Stretching up ('your branches').

Aspect 3: Standing very still and singing the song quietly.

Reluctant children

If a child is reluctant, simply be content to help them stretch their arms (branches) up. If and when they are achieving that, then begin to work on the feet. There are so many benefits from this posture, so do persevere.

Stick

Not only does **Stick** help to stretch and straighten the spine and shoulders, it also gives children the proof that they can be still and quiet and in control. **Stick** also starts and finishes the **Sun Sequences**.

Games for this posture

Umbrella Game, Don't Be Sad, Sneaky Trees, Hoop Game, Spin the Posture, What's the Time, Mr Wolf? Stick **features very much in** *Sun Game* **and** *Sun Sequence*.

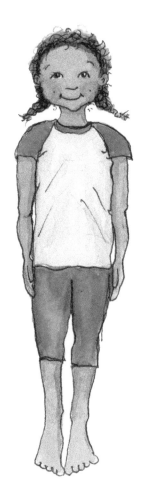

Goals

- *Can I stand with my feet together?*
- *Can I keep my arms by my side?*
- *Can I stand in Stick for the count of ten?*

Resources

None.

What to do

There are several ways to practise this posture.

- Challenge the children to stand in *Stick Posture* with feet together and arms by their sides while you count to ten.
- As above, counting quietly in your mind.
- Use a ten-second timer, progressing to longer times.

Modifications and teaching tips

Such a simple posture can be challenging for children in Maple Group, because being still and quiet can be such a big ask. Try holding their arms by their sides.

Reluctant children

If a child is reluctant to stand in *Stick*, try encouraging them to stand on something specific like a coloured base circle, or a shape. Persevere, because the benefits of a child being able to stand still are obvious.

Teaching Yoga to Children with ASD in Mainstream Primary

Teaching children with ASD in mainstream primary school presents a different set of challenges compared with teaching such children in special schools.

In mainstream you could be teaching:

- whole classes of around 30 children, which may have one or two children on the autism spectrum

- dedicated smaller groups of perhaps ten children with special needs, which may include a mixture of children with ASD and other learning difficulties, and potentially some children with challenging behaviours

- or both!

Whether you are teaching whole classes or smaller groups, your responsibility is to make sure that everyone is involved, engaged and benefits from the lesson. In my opinion, whole classes are the most challenging, and are, frankly, my preferred choice. This is because:

- I love the challenge

- my philosophy is that neurotypical children and children with ASD can experience and learn tolerance, empathy, respect and exemplary behaviours by working together.

So the burning question is: in the whole-class scenario, how do you ensure that children with ASD are included *and* the rest of the class are challenged?

There are three answers to that question:

1. For your own sanity and self-esteem, remember that you can only do your best and there will be times when not every child, ASD or otherwise, will be included for all kinds of reasons, many of which have nothing to do with your teaching ability.

2. It takes time, thoughtful planning, persistence, some creative strategies and often a bit of luck to get to the point when children with ASD are included in the lesson. That's *the goal*, and every step takes you nearer to it.

3. There are stages of my structure that are more 'ASD friendly' than others. This means that you can use those stages as *entry points* for children with ASD while at the same time teaching the rest of the class.

Those 'ASD friendly' entry-points are:

- Sequence stage

- Relaxation stage.

That does not mean that other stages of the lesson should not be used with children with ASD. By all means try to engage them in all stages as the 'Robert' and 'Buddy' case studies illustrate later in the book. I must stress that I have had great success using Sequence and Relaxation stages as entry points and that success was achieved over patient weeks and months as the 'Taz', 'Tommy' and 'Angel' case studies show.

The lesson structure for Oak and Willow Groups (Table 2, page 25) is the structure that I invariably use with primary mainstream classes. You will notice that it is the same structure that I recommend that you use with more able ASD children. Arrows indicate ASD-friendly entry points. You can discover more about the structure that I use in primary schools in my book *Sitting on a Chicken. The Best EVER 52 Yoga Games to Play in School* (see References on page 33).

Table 3: ASD friendly entry points for primary school yoga teaching

LESSON PLAN D		
Stage	Game/Activity	Timing (mins)
Beginning	Good Sitting	2
Sequence	Sun Game	5
Main activity	Shark Game	8
Calming	Rainstick	5
Relaxation	Ladybird Relaxation	5
Plenary	Point to the game you liked best	3
Ending and exit	Bird, then lining up in Stick, quietly waiting to go back to class	2

ASD-FRIENDLY ENTRY POINTS

Case Studies

Here are some case studies that show how the ASD-friendly stages can be used in primary mainstream and how working with my tight structure will help engage children with autism.

'Taz' in Sun Game

'Taz' was eight years old when he suddenly appeared in a Year 3 class a few weeks into the academic year. He was placed in mainstream education because he was waiting for a place in a special school. He had challenging, complex sensory, behavioural and communication needs and was non-verbal. Taz had a learning support assistant (LSA) with him for most of the school day. Taz would come into yoga with his LSA.

We had been practising *Sun Sequence* three weeks prior to Taz's arrival. I realized immediately that *Sun Sequence* would be a step too far for Taz, so I switched to *Sun Game*. Taz's LSA helped him through each part of the sequence, literally moving him into the various postures. It was not easy because he was a big boy. Nevertheless, we all persevered and, little by little, week by week, Taz did more of *Sun Game* independently.

Eventually, by the end of the summer term he actually led the class in *Sun Game*, albeit without speaking. We adults wept tears of happiness and the whole class clapped their hands until they were red.

Taz is an extreme example. However, I have taught countless ASD children with a range of abilities in mainstream who thrived in the sequence section because of the structure, simplicity and repetition.

Monty was a Year 1 pupil (six years old) at a primary school where I teach yoga.

In addition to Monty being non-verbal, he had complex needs including being unable to stay or sit still for long. He would wander where he wanted to, pick up anything he fancied and would scream and laugh loudly for no apparent reason. Here is a short account of what we did and what happened.

Lesson 1

Monty came in with his class and ran around the hall screaming. He was not able to be still or sit in *Good Sitting*. Eventually, he was encouraged to sit on a bench to watch. After five minutes he wanted to leave so his LSA took him out.

Lesson 2

A week later we arranged for Monty to come into an empty hall with his LSA a few minutes before his class. As he had the place to himself he was able to familiarize himself not only with me but also with the surroundings. He ran around the circle of mats, very excited, screaming, yet happy.

A few minutes later his class came into the hall in a very orderly and quiet fashion, as per my expectations. They were not affected by Monty's behaviour because they understood that he behaved that way, because he had special needs. The class was familiar with the structure of the lesson. They were reminded of it by the visual timetable, so they knew what they would be doing.

While we got on with the lesson, Monty walked around the hall making indistinct sounds, sometimes sitting on a bench, but not spoiling the lesson. We got to the Sequence stage when we practised *Sun Game*. The whole class was in a circle practising *Sun Game* together. It was compelling. Monty seemed curious; he joined in with some of the movements. He was excited; he was having fun. His LSA helped him with some of the moves. He was engaged. We were ecstatic. We did the sequence again. Monty joined in the first four movements, then ran out of the hall and did not appear for the rest of the lesson. I thought to myself, 'That is a huge step'. We carried on with the lesson.

Lesson 3

At the start of the lesson, a week later, Monty came in with his class. At first he ran around the hall but eventually his LSA helped him to sit on a bench to watch. He was fairly quiet, watching. The time came for *Sun Game*. Monty got up, came to the mat and with the help of his LSA completed all the stages of *Sun Game*. We all thought that this was amazing.

As the weeks go by, Monty is more engaged in the lesson.

'Buddy' from nursery

Buddy was in a nursery class attached to a primary (elementary) school where I teach. Buddy was four years old, pre-verbal and had complex needs. This is an account of a lesson that I taught his class.

The lesson took place in the school hall on mats. I had been teaching this nursery class since September and it was now mid-March. Buddy came into the lesson with his class. He was accompanied by his LSA. He was encouraged to sit quietly in *Good Sitting* on a mat, as were the rest of the class, and he does so without a fuss.

I waved at Buddy and said hello and he waved back. He looked happy and relaxed.

I held up the *Umbrella Game* card and asked the children to tell me what we were going to play. Most responded 'Umbrella Game'. I showed the card to Buddy and he pointed to the card. We encouraged him to sound the first letter: 'U'. He sounded 'U'.

In *Umbrella Game*, we practised *Chips, Banana, Hero* and *Candle*. He seemed to grasp the jumping element of *Chips*, but needed help from his LSA in stretching and spreading his arms up above his head. Similarly, in *Banana Posture* he needed help stretching his arms above his head. By the end of *Umbrella Game* he had practised all four postures.

We proceeded to the Sequence stage where we played *Sun Game*. There were *ten* parts to this sequence, and Buddy performed *seven* parts of it independently. Buddy's LSA helped him where necessary, which, coincidently, were the postures where arms had to be above the head.

Rainstick Game was next. He was aware that he needed to close his eyes to be chosen. He covered his eyes with his hands, occasionally peeping to see what was going on – but this is what most of the other children do too!

At the end of each stage, the class and I said, for example, 'Rainstick is finished', signing the word finished at the same time. Buddy joined in with this, trying to say 'Finished'.

Finally, it was time for *Bird*, which is the Relaxation stage of the lesson. With minimal help from his LSA, Buddy curled down into *Bird* and stayed very still and quiet in the posture for about three minutes, until he was tapped on the shoulder. This was the signal to come out of the posture, put on shoes and socks and line up by the door of the hall.

Buddy and his class lined up. Before they returned to the classroom some of the children were chosen to point at the visual timetable and say out loud what they enjoyed most. They see it as a real treat, and compete to be chosen.

Buddy pointed to the *Good Sitting* posture card. His LSA modelled the words 'Good Sitting' and Buddy responded by staying 'Sitting'. We all clapped and cheered.

I waved to Buddy as he filed out with his class, and he waved back. He continued to look happy and relaxed.

'Robert's' behaviours

I taught yoga to Robert when he was in nursery, then in Reception and then in Year 1. Robert was Eastern European, very able, highly intelligent, and at the expected language stage of his development but also presented eccentric behaviours and was probably high on the autism spectrum.

Invariably, Robert came into the lesson and was immediately upset because he could not find a *blue* mat. He insisted on having a *blue* mat. Sometimes I 'reserved' a blue mat for him, and other times I encouraged him to stay calm and to ask another child politely if he could have their blue mat.

Robert spent a lot of the lesson trying to get my attention. The kinds of behaviours that he presented were: talking very loudly, singing, waving (at me) and spinning. That said, he was always keen to take on leadership opportunities, for example, leading *Sun Game* or demonstrating a posture to the class. If I chose him he was very happy, but that did not necessarily stop his behaviours. If I *did not* choose him, he was very quick to show his dissatisfaction with me, and would often spend some of the lesson sulking or moaning and sometimes refusing to participate. Often, he confronted me at the end of lesson to tell me that I never chose him and it was 'not fair'.

Of course, Robert was one of 30 children. My responsibility was to *all* the children in the class. It was not the 'Robert' lesson. I saw the behaviours and moaning as part of his behaviour pattern and most times I ignored it.

'Angel' is always on the move

Angel, who was in Year 3 in primary school, showed similar behaviours to Taz, Monty, Buddy and Robert, but above all she found it very difficult to be still. My breakthrough came in the Relaxation stage, using *Ladybird Relaxation*.

You can find *Ladybird Relaxation* in *Ladybird's Remarkable Relaxation* (Chissick and Peacock 2016). Briefly, it is the Relaxation stage of the lesson with the children laying on their backs on their mats while the ladybird lands on specific body parts, for example, big toe, knee, thumb and so on in a sequential, circuit-like order. The incentive is that the ladybird will only choose a child who

(a) has their eyes gently closed, (b) has their arms by their sides and (c) is very still.

Angel was not able to do any of those three things.

I gave Angel's LSA a large ladybird glove puppet, which she showed to Angel and allowed Angel to play with for a little while. Frankly, it is so cute and cuddly that no one, including adults, can resist it, which is part of the plan. The idea was for the LSA to encourage Angel to do a, b and c, or least one of them, while placing the ladybird on the respective body part at the appropriate time.

For any number of reasons, Angel was having none of it. So I asked Angel and her LSA if they would like to be the 'ladybird person' for Mia, the child on the next mat. Angel and her LSA gently placed the puppet on Mia's big toe, knee and so on at the appropriate time. In this way, Angel could see how still Mia remained and that Mia's eyes stayed closed, and the route that the ladybird took and how the whole thing worked.

The following week at the same stage in the lesson we asked Angel if she wanted to be the 'ladybird person' to help Mia or if she would like to lie down like Mia. (I hope you can see where I was going with this.) She chose to be the 'ladybird person' again and did the job without the help of her LSA.

This scenario was played out over the next couple of lessons. Eventually, she agreed to lie down as long as Mia was the 'ladybird person'. Angel lay on her back, arms by her side, occasionally having a little peep to make sure that Mia was there. That was a massive step. Over the ensuing weeks, we built on that until several weeks down the line Angel was performing *Ladybird Relaxation* with the rest of the class.

'Mikey's' sudden appearance

Mikey's case study illustrates the point that whatever the teaching environment, you need to go in with several plans up your sleeve and be ready to switch plan in the wink of an eye.

It was summer term, the beginning of June and the last part of the academic year. This was the nursery class. At the beginning of the year in the autumn term, we had 'played' *Umbrella Game* and *Sun Game* and our Relaxation stage was *Bird*. By the spring term, we had moved on to slightly more challenging games like *Don't Be Sad* and I had introduced *Ladybird Relaxation* and *Rainstick*. The class was doing really well and was ready to move up to more demanding activities and I had planned accordingly.

That day, the nursery class came in normally and the children sat on mats in *Good Sitting*. Suddenly, and without any warning, Mikey appeared in the hall squashed between two senior teaching assistants. Mikey had a lovely smile on his face, so I knew he was not in any discomfort, and apart from the shouting he seemed quite happy to see me. I had never met him before, although I had heard that they had not brought him into yoga because he was so difficult to manage.

'Let's give it a go,' said 'Sally' the nursery teacher. 'See how long he can stay in the hall. If it gets too much we'll take him back to the classroom.'

Immediately, I changed the visual timetable to reflect the lesson that I had taught in the autumn term, starting with *Umbrella Game*, then *Sun Game* and finally *Bird*. Luckily, I keep the umbrella in my resources bag. I also upped my game and taught at an increased pace, with limitless enthusiasm, and kept my verbal input to the absolute minimum. As a result, Mikey was totally engaged in all stages of the lesson, even curling down quietly in *Bird*. To say that the teaching staff were delighted would be an understatement. Not a dry eye in the house! The rest of the class loved revisiting the activities and enjoyed Mikey being involved in an activity rather than disrupting it. A successful lesson all round.

In fairness, I cannot take all the credit. I discovered later that the nursery had set up a yoga studio in their classroom several weeks before. It was a small area that consisted of three yoga mats and a display of posture cards and game cards that we had used in our lessons. Children were encouraged to 'play' yoga in the 'studio' along with other options that the classroom offered, like, for example, the dressing-up box or the sand-play area. We could not be 100 per cent sure, but there was a general consensus that Mikey had seen his classmates in *Chips*, *Candle*, *Hero* and *Banana Postures* and was more familiar with the lesson than anyone realized.

Reference

Chissick, M. and Peacock, S. (2016) *Ladybird's Remarkable Relaxation*. London: Jessica Kingsley Publishers.

Resources

Great resources are essential for great lessons. I urge you to equip yourself with the best resources that you can afford. Here are details of my posture cards, game cards and songs to accompany the games, all of which have been painstakingly developed over many years.

Posture and game cards

Using visuals is fundamental when teaching yoga to children with autism. The visual timetable, which displays posture cards and game cards, is integral to my teaching approach and will, without doubt, improve the children's engagement and your classroom management enormously.

Here is the *Tree Posture* card together with the *Crown Game* and *Shark Game* cards.

crown game

© Copyright Yoga At School 2016

shark game

© Copyright Yoga At School 2016

tree

©Copyright Yoga At School Ltd 2014

You can make your own posture or game cards or you could save a lot of time, energy and at the same time present yourself more professionally by downloading mine at: www.yogaatschool.org. uk/autism.

As you have bought this book you are entitled to a discount. Your **discount code** is: ASD100

Songs for games

You do not need to reinvent the wheel in terms of the songs. You can access and download them at the same website page. Again, use the same code ASD200 to obtain them for free.

Animation video: yoga session for children with autism

In this explainer training video, a cartoon version of me, with help from a very special guest, takes you through a whole session, which is the Universal Lesson Plan A.

You will be able to see the structure and stages of the session *in action*: the teaching approach, how to engage children in the session, which postures to teach, *how* to teach them, *when* to teach them and *where* to teach them.

You will also see cartoon versions of children in the postures and learn how to get the best from adult support. In addition, you will learn which resources to use, how to set up for the lesson, how to encourage the reluctant child; and, most importantly, how to make the session fun and impactful.

You can download the video at www.yogaatschool.org.uk/autism and use the **discount code:** ASD300

Other resources

If you would like guidance on other resources for children's yoga, feel free to contact me at: info@yogaatschool.org.uk.

Posture cards and games cards to start you off

To start you off, here is the *Umbrella Game* card together with small posture cards for the same game, which you can copy, laminate and use immediately.

Have fun!

umbrella game

© Copyright Yoga At School 2016

hero

boat

banana

dragon

candle

frog

chips

tree

Easy Ways to Choose Games and Postures

Games list

Banana Game
Bird
Circles Game
Crown Game
Don't Be Sad
Hoop Game
Ladybird Relaxation
Rainstick Game
Shark Game
Sneaky Trees
Spin the Posture
Umbrella Game
What's the Time, Mr Wolf?

Games by ability group

Maple Group
Sneaky Trees
Spin the Posture
Umbrella Game
What's the Time, Mr Wolf?

Oak Group

Banana Game
Bird
Circles Game
Crown Game
Don't Be Sad
Hoop Game
Ladybird Relaxation
Rainstick Game
Shark Game
Sneaky Trees
Spin the Posture
Umbrella Game
What's the Time, Mr Wolf?

Willow Group

Banana Game
Bird
Circles Game
Crown Game
Don't Be Sad
Hoop Game
Ladybird Relaxation
Rainstick Game
Shark Game
Sneaky Trees
Spin the Posture
Umbrella Game
What's the Time, Mr Wolf?

Postures

Banana
Boat
Candle
Chips

Dragon
Frog
Good Sitting
Hero
Tree